# Margot Robbie

## Bold *Barbie* Actress & Producer

by Grace Hansen

Abdo Kids Jumbo is an Imprint of Abdo Kids
abdobooks.com

**abdobooks.com**

Published by Abdo Kids, a division of ABDO, P.O. Box 398166, Minneapolis, Minnesota 55439.


Printed in the United States of America, North Mankato, Minnesota.

052024

092024

Photo Credits: Alamy, Everette Collection, Getty Images, Shutterstock

Production Contributors: Teddy Borth, Jennie Forsberg, Grace Hansen
Design Contributors: Candice Keimig, Pakou Moua

Library of Congress Control Number: 2023948672

Publisher's Cataloging-in-Publication Data

Names: Hansen, Grace, author.

Title: Margot Robbie: bold Barbie actress & producer / by Grace Hansen

Other title: bold Barbie actress & producer

Description: Minneapolis, Minnesota : Abdo Kids, 2025 | Series: Leading biographies | Includes online resources and index.

Identifiers: ISBN 9798384900764 (lib. bdg.) | ISBN 9798384901464 (ebook) | ISBN 9798384901815 (Read-to-me eBook)

Subjects: LCSH: Robbie, Margot, 1990---Juvenile literature. | Motion picture actors and actresses--Biography--Juvenile literature. | Actresses--Biography--Juvenile literature. | Barbie (Fictitious character)--Juvenile literature. | Motion picture producers and directors--Biography--Juvenile literature.

Classification: DDC 791.43092--dc23

# Table of Contents


Margot's Beginnings . . . . . . . . . . . 4

The Acting Scene. . . . . . . . . . . . . . 8

Barbie!. . . . . . . . . . . . . . . . . . . . . . 16

Bigger than Barbie . . . . . . . . . . . 20

Career Highlights. . . . . . . . . . . . . 22

Glossary . . . . . . . . . . . . . . . . . . . . 23

Index . . . . . . . . . . . . . . . . . . . . . . . 24

Abdo Kids Code. . . . . . . . . . . . . . 24

## Margot's Beginnings

Margot Elise Robbie was born on July 2, 1990, in Dalby, Queensland, Australia. Margot and her three siblings were raised by their mother.

Queensland
Dalby
Australia

## The Acting Scene

Margot studied **drama** in high school. She worked to earn money to support her dreams. After graduation, Margot moved to Melbourne to act.

In 2008, Margot was **cast** as Donna Freedman in the **soap opera** *Neighbors*. She became well known throughout Australia for this role.

ATTENTION
ALL
STAFF

In 2010, Margot left *Neighbors*. She moved to Hollywood, California, to act in her first American TV show. In 2013, Margot starred in her first **blockbuster** film. This launched her Hollywood career!

In 2016, Margot played DC Comics villain Harley Quinn. She was the first actor to portray the character in film. Margot performed many of her own stunts.

Daddy's
Lil Monste

## Barbie!

In 2018, Margot began working as a **producer** for the film *Barbie*. Margot hired Greta Gerwig to write and direct the film.

After another actress declined to play Barbie, Margot took on the role herself! *Barbie* hit theaters on July 9, 2023. It went on to become the **highest-grossing** film of the year.

10:16:16
14R
TAKE
6 P/U
100
1/2 SFX
Barbie
Camera
Rodrigo Prieto
ASC AMC

## Bigger than Barbie

Margot has wowed fans for years with her acting range. People can only guess what roles she will take on next.

# Career Highlights

**2014** Margot co-founds the production company LuckyChap Entertainment.

**2016** Margot hosts *Saturday Night Live*.

**2017** Margot produces and stars in the film *I, Tonya*.

**January 2018** Margot receives her first Academy Award nomination for Best Actress for her role as Tonya Harding in *I, Tonya*.

**February 2018** Margot narrates for and voice acts in the film *Peter Rabbit*.

**2019** Margot is nominated for several awards for Best Supporting Actress for her role in the film *Bombshell*.

**July 2019** Margot plays late actress Sharon Tate in the Academy Award-winning film *Once Upon a Time in Hollywood*.

**2023** *Barbie* earns $1.44 billion to become the 14th **highest-grossing** film of all time.

# Glossary

**blockbuster** – a film with an extremely high production and marketing budget.

**cast** – to be chosen for a part in a play or film.

**drama** – a television show or film that is serious in nature and reveals emotional conflicts among fictional characters.

**highest-grossing** – earning more money than other similar things.

**producer** – a person who plans and coordinates various aspects of film production, such as selecting the script, coordinating writing, directing, editing, and arranging financing.

**soap opera** – a television drama series dealing typically with daily events in the lives of the same group of characters.

**trapeze** – a rope swing with a bar hung high above the ground. A trapeze is often used by acrobats in a circus.

# Index


*Barbie* 16, 18

birth 4

childhood 4, 6

Dalby, Queensland, Australia 4

education 8

family 4

film 12, 14, 16, 18

Gerwig, Greta 16

Harley Quinn 14

Melbourne, Australia 8

*Neighbors* 10, 12

television 10, 12

United States 12